ASTERIX AND THE GOLDEN SICKLE

TEXT BY GOSCINNY

DRAWINGS BY UDERZO

TRANSLATED BY ANTHEA BELL AND DEREK HOCKRIDGE

HODDER DARGAUD

LONDON SYDNEY AUCKLAND

ASTERIX IN OTHER COUNTRIES

Australia Hodder Dargaud, Rydalmere Business Park, 10/16 South Street, Rydalmere, N.S.W. 2116, Australia

Austria Delta Verlag, Postfach 10 12 45, 7000 Stuttgart 1, Germany

Belgium Dargaud Bénélux, 3 rue Kindermans, 1050 Brussels, Belgium

Brazil Record Distribuidora, Rua Argentina 171, 20921 Rio de Janeiro, Brazil

Canada (French) Dargaud Canada, Presse-Import, 307 Benjamin Hudon, St Laurent, Montreal, Quebec H4N 1J1, Canada
(English) General Publishing Co. Ltd, 30 Lesmill Road, Don Mills, Ontario M38 2T6, Canada

Denmark Serieforlaget A/S (Gutenberghus Group), Vognmagergade 11, 1148 Copenhagen K, Denmark

Finland Sanoma Corporation, P.O. Box 107, 00381 Helsinki 38, Finland

France Dargaud Editeur, 6 Rue Gager-Gabillot, 75015 Paris, France
(titles up to and including Asterix in Belgium)
Les Editions Albert René, 26 Avenue Victor Hugo, 75116 Paris, France
(titles from Asterix and the Great Divide onwards)

Germany Delta Verlag, Postfach 10 12 45, 7000 Stuttgart 1, Germany

Greece Mamouth Comix Ltd, Ippokratous 57, 106080 Athens, Greece

Holland Dargaud Bénélux, 3 rue Kindermans, 1050 Brussels, Belgium
(Distribution) Betapress, Burg. Krollaan 14, 5126 PT, Jilze, Holland

Hong Kong Hodder Dargaud, c/o Publishers Associates Ltd, 11th Floor, Taikoo Trading Estate, 28 Tong Cheong Street, Quarry Bay, Hong Kong

Hungary Egmont Pannonia, Pannonhalmi ut. 14, 1118 Budapest, Hungary

Indonesia Penerbit Sinar Harapan, J1. Dewi Sartika 136D, Jakarta Cawang, Indonesia

Italy Mondadori, Via Belvedere, 37131 Verona, Italy

Latin America Grijalbo-Dargaud S.A., Aragon 385, 08013 Barcelona, Spain

Luxemburg Imprimerie St. Paul, rue Christophe Plantin 2, Luxemburg

New Zealand Hodder Dargaud, P.O. Box 3858, Auckland 1, New Zealand

Norway A/S Hjemmet (Gutenburghus Group), Kristian den 4des gt. 13, Oslo 1, Norway

Portugal Meriberica-Liber, Avenida Duque d'Avila 69, R/C esq., 1000 Lisbon, Portugal

Roman Empire (Latin) Delta Verlag, Postfach 10 12 45, 7000 Stuttgart 1, Germany

Southern Africa Hodder Dargaud, c/o Struik Book Distributors (Pty) Ltd, Graph Avenue, Montague Gardens 7441, South Africa

Spain Grijalbo-Dargaud S.A., Aragon 385, 08013 Barcelona, Spain

Sweden Hemmets Journal (Gutenberghus Group), Fack, 200 22 Malmö, Sweden

Switzerland Dargaud (Suisse) S.A., En Budron B, 1052 Le Mont sur Lausanne, Switzerland

Wales (Welsh) Gwasg Y Dref Wen, 28 Church Road, Whitchurch, Cardiff, Wales

Yugoslavia Nip Forum, Vojvode Misica 1-3, 2100 Novi Sad, Yugoslavia

Asterix and the Golden Sickle

ISBN 0 340 20209 2 (cased)
ISBN 0 340 21209 8 (limp)

Copyright © Dargaud Editeur 1962, Goscinny-Uderzo
English language text copyright © Hodder and Stoughton Ltd 1975

First published in Great Britain 1975 (cased)
This impression 93 94 95 96

First published in Great Britain 1977 (limp)
This impression 93 94 95 96

Published by Hodder Dargaud Ltd,
Mill Road, Dunton Green, Sevenoaks, Kent TN13 2YA

Printed in Belgium by Proost International Book Production

GAULISH VILLAGE

COMPENDIUM

LAUDANUM

AQUARIUM

TOTORUM

ARMORICA

BELGICA

LUTETIA

SPQR

GAUL

(ROMAN CONQUEST)
50 B.C.

CELTICA

PROVINCIA

AQUITANIA

he year is 50 BC. Gaul is entirely occupied by the Romans.
ell, not entirely… One small village of indomitable Gauls still
olds out against the invaders. And life is not easy for the
oman legionaries who garrison the fortified camps of
otorum, Aquarium, Laudanum and Compendium…

a few of the Gauls

Asterix, the hero of these adventures. A shrewd, cunning little warrior; all perilous missions are immediately entrusted to him. Asterix gets his superhuman strength from the magic potion brewed by the druid Getafix…

Obelix, Asterix's inseparable friend. A menhir delivery-man by trade; addicted to wild boar. Obelix is always ready to drop everything and go off on a new adventure with Asterix — so long as there's wild boar to eat, and plenty of fighting.

Getafix, the venerable village druid. Gathers mistletoe and brews magic potions. His speciality is the potion which gives the drinker superhuman strength. But Getafix also has other recipes up his sleeve…

Cacofonix, the bard. Opinion is divided as to his musical gifts. Cacofonix thinks he's a genius. Everyone else thinks he's unspeakable. But so long as he doesn't speak, let alone sing, everybody likes him…

Finally, Vitalstatistix, the chief of the tribe. Majestic, brave and hot-tempered, the old warrior is respected by his men and feared by his enemies. Vitalstatistix himself has only one fear; he is afraid the sky may fall on his head tomorrow. But as he always says, 'Tomorrow never comes.'

Asterix and the Golden Sickle

THE FIERCELY INDEPENDENT LITTLE VILLAGE WHERE ASTERIX AND THE OTHER GAULS LIVE IS AT PEACE...

GOOD HUNTING, ASTERIX?

NOTHING MUCH TODAY...

OBELIX IS HAPPILY AT WORK, CARVING OUT A MENHIR...

THERE'LL ALWAYS BE A GAU-AAUL!!!

CACOFONIX THE BARD IS GIVING THE CHILDREN LESSONS...

WELL, YOUNG MAN, AND INTO HOW MANY PARTS IS GAUL DIVIDED?

?

$$VIII \times V = XL$$

$$\frac{III}{+ \ \ I} = \frac{I}{IV}$$

IN SHORT, EVERYONE IS CONTENTED. ALL IS PEACE AND PLENTY...

ANOTHER BOAR, OBELIX?

YES, PLEASE!

WHEN SUDDENLY...

OH, BY TOUTATIS!

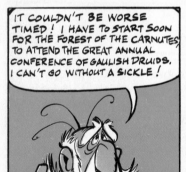

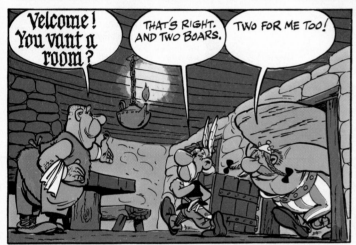

9

14

SO SORRY. HOW CLUMSY OF ME!

DON'T MENTION IT!

IT WAS NOTHING!

YOU LOOK LIKE STRANGERS TO OUR GREAT CITY. PERHAPS I CAN HELP YOU?

WE'RE LOOKING FOR METALLURGIX...

METALLURGIX? WHY HE'S MY BEST FRIEND! AND WHAT DO YOU WANT HIM FOR?

WHAT A LUCKY COINCIDENCE!

WE WANT TO BUY A GOLDEN SICKLE FROM HIM.

EXCELLENT, EXCELLENT!

METALLURGIX HAS RETIRED AND LEFT LUTETIA.

OH DEAR!

BUT NEVER MIND. YOU COME WITH ME. I CAN GET YOU A SICKLE AT A VERY COMPETITIVE PRICE!

WELL, THE THING IS...

AND WHAT AM I GOING TO DO WITH MY MENHIR?

WOULD YOU LIKE TO LEAVE YOUR THINGS?

CLOAKS

21

THE SUN, RISING ON LUTETIA, IS GREETED BY A COCKEREL....

COCK-A-DOODLE-DO!

GET UP, OBELIX! IT'S TIME TO START OUR INVESTIGATIONS!

THAT'S RIGHT. WE MUST FIND METALLURGIX.

LET'S GO BACK TO THAT ARVERNIAN IN THE WINE SHOP. I'M SURE HE KNOWS SOMETHING!

THE SUN OF MASSILIA

OH!

COULD YOU TELL US WHERE TO FIND THE ARVERNIAN WHO....

OH, I EXPECT YOU MEAN THE FORMER PROPRIETOR?

THAT CRAZY GAUL WHO SOLD ME THIS PLACE FOR A HANDFUL OF BRONZE COINS! IT'S UNDER NEW MANAGEMENT NOW, BUT YOU WON'T BE DISAPPOINTED!

I CAN OFFER YOU MY SPECIALITY: FISH SOUP! MADE OF NICE FRESH FISH, JUST ARRIVED BY OX-CART FROM MASSILIA!

DO YOU KNOW WHERE THE ARVERNIAN HAS GONE?

OH! HE STARTED FOR GERGOVIA THIS MORNING, TRAVELLING BY OX-CART, THE SAME AS THE FISH!

THE SUN OF MASSILIA

WHAT A SHAME! IF YOU'D COME A LITTLE SOONER YOU'D HAVE FOUND HIM STILL HERE!

THANKS!

ALL THESE LUTETIANS ARE CRAZY, BY BELISAMA!

18

THE ARVERNIAN! IN FRONT THERE!

LET'S GO!

AND THE GREAT RACE IS ON!

GEE UP! GEE UP!

I'M GOING TO OVERTAKE!

BONG!

WHAT'S THE MATTER? WHAT DO YOU WANT?

WHERE'S METALLURGIX? TELL US ALL YOU KNOW!

NOT TALKING, EH?

STOP! STOP!

LEAVE HIM TO ME, ASTERIX! LET ME HAVE A GO!

ONE DAY SOME MEN CAME AND TOOK METALLURGIX AWAY... I HAPPENED TO BE PASSING, AND THEY WERE GOING TO TAKE ME TOO...

BUT ONE OF THE MEN, CALLED CLOVOGARLIX, LET ME GO ON CONDITION I TOLD HIM IF ANYONE CAME LOOKING FOR METALLURGIX. THEY FORCED ME TO BE THEIR ACCOMPLICE, BUT I'M INNOCENT REALLY!

RIGHT! THE ARVERNIAN HAS GIVEN US CLOVOGARLIX'S ADDRESS... WE'LL GO THERE!

WE OUGHT TO HAVE KEPT ONE OF THE OXEN FOR A SNACK...

I'LL NEVER SET FOOT IN LUTETIA AGAIN!

20

24

27

28

THE SUN GOD, BELENOS HIMSELF, IS SHOWING US THE WAY!

THAT'S NICE OF HIM!

YOU'RE NOT AFRAID OF COMING ACROSS WOLVES, ARE YOU?

NO, BUT I HOPE WE COME ACROSS SOME BOARS AS WELL, BECAUSE I'M HUNGRY AND I DON'T LIKE WOLF...

WE'LL PROBABLY COME ACROSS BANDITS TOO!

NO, THANKS, I DON'T FANCY BANDIT EITHER.

OUR TWO FRIENDS MAKE THEIR WAY TOWARDS THE THICK FOREST, AS YET UNAWARE THAT IT WILL BECOME THE BOIS DE BOULOGNE...

WHERE ARE YOU OFF TO?

THE FOREST!

THE FOREST'S DANGEROUS AT NIGHT, WHAT WITH WOLVES AND BANDITS!

HUH! WE GAULS DON'T KNOW THE MEANING OF FEAR!

SPEAK FOR YOURSELVES! I'M A GAUL, AND I'M AFRAID!

WHICH SHALL WE COME ACROSS FIRST, WOLVES OR BANDITS?

SHALL WE HAVE A BET?

IF IT'S WOLVES, YOU BUY A ROUND OF BEER, IF IT'S BANDITS I WILL.

DONE!

SLAP!

HOUOUOUOUOUOU

WOLVES! I'VE WON!

BEASTLY ANIMALS!

POC!

30

31

WARM RAYS OF BRILLIANT SUNSHINE LIGHT UP A CLOUDLESS SKY...

... LITTLE BIRDS WARBLE ON THE LEAFY BRANCHES ...

... SQUIRRELS PLAY ON THE MOSSY GROUND ...

... WHILE UNDERNEATH THE MOSSY GROUND...

GET THEM OBELIX!

YOU BET I WILL, ASTERIX!

BOING PLAF! OUCH! BOUM!

ARE THERE ANY LEFT, ASTERIX?

NO, OBELIX, YOU'RE JUST FINISHING OFF THE LAST ONE...

BONG! BONG! BONG!

LET'S GET OUT OF HERE AND WARN THE BOSS!

OBELIX, I'M A BIT WORRIED... I CAN'T FIND NAVISHTRIX!

HE CAN'T HAVE COME TO ANY HARM, HE WAS HERE JUST NOW!

ANYWAY, I'VE GOT CLOVOGARLIX.

THAT'S SOMETHING...

37

40

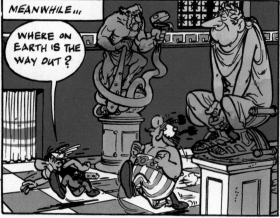

43

PRINTED IN BELGIUM BY

proost

INTERNATIONAL BOOK PRODUCTION